Harriet Tubman

Callie Smith Grant

Illustrated by
Ken Landgraf

BARBOUR
PUBLISHING, I
Uhrichsville, Ohio

D0249595

© MCMXCIX by Barbour Publishing, Inc.

ISBN 1-57748-651-X

Published by Barbour Publishing, Inc., P.O. Box 719, Uhrichsville, Ohio 44683 http://www.barbourbooks.com

ecpa Member of the
Evangelical Christian
Publishers Association

Printed in the United States of America.

Harriet Tubman

AN OLD WOMAN SAT IN A ROCKING CHAIR.

Prologue

Inside a slave cabin on the eastern shore of the state of Maryland, an old woman sat in a rocking chair and stared into the fire crackling in her small fireplace. She remembered tending it carefully only a few hours earlier as she cooked a huge Christmas dinner for her grown children.

This was the time of year when slaves had a few days off from the work that consumed their bodies and crushed their spirits. She was sure most of her children would come home from the nearby plantations where they worked and spend the holiday with their parents. That's how they had celebrated Christmas for years, so why should 1854 be any different?

She'd killed and roasted a pig and cooked up her children's favorite foods. Then she'd waited all day for them. Even her husband had taken to looking out the door from time to time.

But dusk was falling, and not one of her children or grandchildren had come. It was clear they weren't coming at all. It was almost more than the old woman could bear. As the fire slowly died away to embers, she rocked back and forth, weeping quietly.

She did not know that four of her grown children were only a few yards away, hiding with other slaves in a shed filled with fodder for livestock.

Her daughter, Harriet Tubman, secretly watched the woman through the open cabin door. The firelight made Momma's face bright, and each tear glistened as it ran down her wrinkled cheeks. Harriet was heartbroken that she could not speak to her momma directly.

EVEN HER HUSBAND WAS LOOKING OUT THE DOOR.

HARRIET TUBMAN

The smells of the carefully prepared dinner tortured the hungry slaves as they hid in the musty building. Waves of homesickness overwhelmed them, and they longed to go to their parents. They remembered the personal warmth of the weathered cabin and the closeness of the small community of slaves who lived around it.

Harriet was the youngest of ten children born to the now-aging couple, Ben and Harriet Ross. She still remembered her early childhood, happy years spent playing on the dirt floor of the cabin. In those days she was known by her baby name, Minty. She was a young woman now, and her life's work was just beginning. For five years, Harriet had secretly helped slaves travel north to freedom. Tomorrow she would be leading more out of bondage in Maryland, and this time some were members of her own family.

They had all come to say good-bye, but as they approached their parents' cabin, Harriet realized the emotional scene created by their announcement

THEY HID IN THE MUSTY BUILDING.

would be noticed. If anyone found them there, it would jeopardize all their lives, including the lives of their parents.

Harriet sighed. She wished they could celebrate the birth of the Baby Jesus all together with the old folks, but she needed these few days without work to put some distance between her runaways and their masters. She wanted them to be far down the road toward freedom before they were missed.

For now, they hid in the shed, resting up for a long, dangerous journey, mostly on foot, through parts of Maryland, Delaware, New Jersey, and into Pennsylvania.

Two of the men, John and Peter, were not related to Harriet. Once darkness fell, they knocked on the cabin door, intending to ask for food. Old Poppa Ross came to the door and stepped outside to talk with the men, leaving his sad wife to stare into the remains of the fire and dab at her eyes with a well-worn apron.

Outside, the men spoke softly. "We're friends of

THE MEN SPOKE SOFTLY.

Harriet's and your boys," they told Poppa. "They didn't come to you 'cause we're heading north. We're in the shed over yonder right now, and your children don't dare come out to be seen. But they want to say good-bye. And we need food real bad."

The old man understood immediately. Calmly, he slipped back into the cabin and spoke to his wife.

Harriet watched from afar. There was no change in her momma's expression. Apparently the old man hadn't told her their children were nearby. Harriet smiled at that wise decision. Momma was apt to start shouting, "Glory!" Besides, if she didn't know they were there, she could honestly say so later on.

Poppa bundled up some food in a gunnysack and followed the other men away from the cabin.

When they got close to the shed, Poppa said, "Blindfold me."

The younger men looked at each other. Was this old man crazy?

"I say blindfold me, and make it tight, young fellas."

POPPA BUNDLED UP SOME FOOD.

One man pulled out his bandana, rolled it into a long strip, and tied it over the old man's eyes. Then they led him into the shed where his children were hiding.

Harriet and her brothers spent time with their father that Christmas Day. They ate and talked, but the old man never took off his blindfold.

The next day, rested and carrying food for the journey, Harriet and the escaping slaves headed north.

Old Poppa knew that when his children were discovered missing, he would be questioned, and Poppa was a devout Christian who would not lie. Sure enough, a few days later, he and Momma were called to the master's house, which everyone called the Big House, for questioning.

Momma knew nothing. "I looked for them all day," she said sadly. "They never did come."

"Did you see your children before they left, old man?" the law asked Poppa.

"No," he said. "I ain't seen my children in months."

THE OLD MAN NEVER TOOK OFF HIS BLINDFOLD.

And it was true. He had talked to his children, he had eaten with them, but he did not "see" them before they escaped to freedom. And he knew he might never see any of them again.

It gave him great satisfaction to know that his beloved little Minty had grown up to become the courageous Harriet Tubman. Her path had been long and hard, but now she acted with the assurance of one watched over by the Lord Himself. Poppa Ross never doubted that she would succeed in escorting her runaways to the safety of Canada. There they would be slaves no more.

But he suspected that Harriet would be back. She had always come back to them before. Even the heavy hand of slavery had not been able to separate her from them for long.

LITTLE MINTY HAD GROWN UP
TO BECOME HARRIET TUBMAN.

MINTY HAD JUST BEEN SOLD.

1

A layer of fog settled over the saltwater marshes of eastern Maryland. Moving slowly through the silver haze was a wagon drawn by one beaten-down old horse. A young white woman held the reins, and tucked in the back sat a six-year-old slave girl called Minty. She shivered in her sack dress in the damp fog. Her soft brown eyes blinked in terror, for Minty had just been sold.

Not an hour before she'd been dragged crying from her momma and poppa, carried screaming from the only home she'd ever known, a slave cabin on the land of Master Edward Brodas in Dorchester County. Now she was on her way to this stranger's house. The woman needed some kind of help with her work at home, but she was not well off. The only slave she and her husband could afford to buy from the master was a child—Minty.

Where's she gonna take me? Minty thought. *What they gonna do with me?* Horrible scenes paraded through her mind, drawn from whispered nighttime conversations she had overheard and only half-remembered or understood. Were white people really ghosts? Would they beat her? Kill her? One frightful image faded into the next as her heart pounded with terror.

In the early 1800s, at the time Minty was born, black people had much to fear in America. Whether they lived in the northern or southern states, most of them were slaves. The few blacks who were free did not have the same rights that most white people took for granted. Even in the North, there were all sorts of restrictions on where they could live, what

WERE WHITE PEOPLE REALLY GHOSTS?

jobs they could hold, and who they could marry.

The southern states had a huge and rapidly increasing population of slaves. As the number of black slaves increased, white people became more and more fearful of a black uprising that would kill thousands of white men, women, and children.

Some white masters didn't like slavery but believed they didn't have any choice about having slaves. The entire southern way of life was dependent on slavery. Life revolved around the huge, wealthy farms called plantations, which grew acres and acres of cotton and tobacco. These plantations needed hundreds of slaves to do all the work. The blacks farmed the land, cared for the livestock, cooked the food, cleaned the clothes, and performed innumerable other tasks for their masters. *Without slaves,* their owners wondered, *how could the plantations survive?*

Slaves owned nothing, not even themselves. Slaves were bought and sold as if they were objects or animals. The life of a slave was full of uncertainty,

THE PLANTATIONS NEEDED HUNDREDS OF SLAVES.

because if the fields did not produce and the master of the plantation did not prosper, he might feel the need to sell some slaves for extra cash. Kinder masters tried to keep families together, but not all masters were kind. Wives were often sold and separated from their husbands. Children like Minty were routinely sold as well. It was a sad day at the plantation when any slave was sold, but when families were split up, the grief was especially great.

Whether a master was kind or not, the life of a slave was one of poverty, fear, and brutally hard work. Slaves were dependent on the generosity of their master for food, clothing, shelter, and medical care. No master was particularly generous in those areas.

Slaves usually lived in one-room shacks with dirt floors and no windows. The cabins were cold in the winter and hot in the summer. The only heat came from a fireplace that smoked up the cabin, and this was where all the cooking was done as well. Most slaves had one outfit to wear—one dress or

SLAVES LIVED IN ONE-ROOM SHACKS.

one pair of pants and a shirt.

The life of a slave was strictly regulated. Slaves could not simply come and go as they pleased. They needed written permission to travel from place to place. They were discouraged from meeting together in large numbers. Even religious meetings in the slave quarters were sometimes frowned upon.

It was illegal to teach a slave to read and write, although the wives and daughters of some plantation owners taught their house slaves to read the Bible. The workday for most slaves stretched from before the sun rose to after it set.

Under such conditions, it was inevitable that some slaves would run away. When they did, they were hunted down like animals, with large packs of dogs. Occasionally, a slave escaped and was never heard from again. Most runaways, however, were quickly recaptured and whipped severely to punish them and to make an example of them so that others would be too frightened to try the same thing. Punishment and the fear of punishment were the

RUNAWAY SLAVES WERE
HUNTED DOWN LIKE ANIMALS.

main weapons white southerners used to maintain their power over the blacks who lived in their midst.

Araminta Ross, as Minty was named at her birth around 1820, had already learned more than she ever wanted to know about this life of slavery, even in the few years she had been alive. One thing she never learned was her birthday, because such records were not normally kept for slaves.

Minty never doubted the love of her parents, who had already lost two other young daughters when their master sold them to a chain gang. Her parents were fiercely determined to protect her as much as possible from the suffering of their bondage. They worked hard to include her in the love of their large family. They taught her about their love for God and encouraged her to think of Jesus as her personal friend.

The entire community of slaves on the plantation helped Minty to find joy in the simple details of daily life and to hope for a better life in the world to come. It seemed this world held a grim future for

SHE THOUGHT OF JESUS AS HER PERSONAL FRIEND.

baby Minty because slave life was so hard. Most of all, they taught her to express her sorrows and hopes in worship to God and to find comfort and inspiration in God's love for her.

Some plantation owners allowed their slaves to gather for church services. Others found any gathering too threatening. The slaves, they feared, would use the time to plan their escape or, even worse, to plot the murder of their masters. Where they were not allowed to worship openly, slaves often met in secret in what they called brush arbors—areas of dense pine thickets where the boughs would absorb sound. Even the fear of the whip could not keep them from praising Jesus out loud.

As Minty bounced along in the wagon, she looked up at the pearl-gray sky and called out to her closest friend. *Oh Jesus, watch over me,* she prayed.

She knew Momma was praying for her at this very minute. She'd heard her momma pray every time a slave disappeared, whether the slave had been sold or was suspected to have run away.

SLAVES OFTEN MET IN SECRET.

"Jesus, protect Your children down here," Momma would pray fervently in the privacy of their one-room cabin. "*Protect* them! Make them strong, make them swift. Make them do right by You. Make them *free*." Then Momma would rock and moan. It was kind of like singing, but it was softer and seemed full of all the hurt in the world.

Until today, Minty had just watched her momma express those deep longings, while praying so hard it seemed likely to tear her soul from her body. But today Minty was learning to make some of those fervent prayers her own. Though Minty was still a child, she had grown years in her understanding of the world around her in just the last few hours.

She thought of the songs she'd heard sung in the slave quarters, songs the masters had decided were too dangerous and might cause a slave to think of freedom and personal dignity. At first, Minty had not been able to figure that out. How could it be dangerous to sing about wanting to go to glory and be with Jesus?

MINTY HAD HEARD THE SLAVES SING.

And what was wrong with singing about the stories in the Bible? Since most slaves could not read, Bible stories were told aloud and sung. Minty loved the songs about Moses leading the Israelites out of Egypt through all kinds of dangers to get to the Promised Land. She'd hear the grown-ups sing from the depths of their souls:

> *If I could I surely would*
> > *Stand on the rock where Moses stood*
> *Pharaoh's army got drown-ded.*
> > *Oh Mary don't you weep.*

Or perhaps they would shout out her favorite:

> *Go down, Moses,*
> > *Way down in Egypt land.*
> *Tell ole Pharaoh*
> > *Let my people go!*

Minty loved the songs. Sometimes they were

MINTY LOVED THE SONGS ABOUT MOSES.

sung softly in the cabin, and sometimes the field hands sang them loud and strong and in unison to help them get through the long day's toil. She knew what the songs were about: A day would come when Jesus would come again to take them away and make everything right. Then the lion would lie down with the lamb and the bondage of slavery would no longer have a hold on them.

Even as a little slip of a girl, Minty understood that slavery was evil. Some Christian masters read their Bibles differently on that topic, and white folks all over the world discussed to no end whether or not slavery should continue to exist. But the slaves knew the good Lord had never intended them to be imprisoned in this life of fear and suffering.

Minty was still a little too young to understand that the songs she loved had a second meaning to black folks. They spoke of freedom. Sometimes they told of being freed from slavery by dying and going on to heaven, and sometimes they told about being alive and taking the actual journey north to liberty.

THE FIELD HANDS SANG IN UNISON.

Minty would hear someone sing, *Oh Canaan, sweet Canaan, I am bound for the land of Canaan,* and the sweet sounds seemed full of mystery to her. She had only recently been able to tell the words Canaan and Canada apart, they felt so alike rolling off her southern tongue. Just last week, Momma had explained that Canaan was the Promised Land in the Bible, but Canada was a snowy land way up north where blacks could not be held as slaves.

"Either one says freedom," Poppa had muttered as he poked at the fire with a stick.

Momma had given him a stern look out of the corner of her eye. "You hush," she scolded gently. Though the cabin felt warm, cozy, and safe, you could never be sure who might be listening outside. And it wouldn't be good to let the master know there was freedom talk going on in the quarters.

Go down, Moses, Minty sang to herself as the wagon slowed. She wrapped her thin brown arms around her body. *Oh Lord, be with me*, she prayed over and over.

SHE WRAPPED HER ARMS AROUND HER BODY.

The wagon turned off onto a narrower dirt road she had never seen before, and Minty felt numb with both cold and fear. A small log house with a fence around it appeared. It didn't look anything like the Big House. It sat in a clearing in the woods, and Minty could smell the river nearby, but she had no idea where she was. She'd never left the Brodases' plantation before and had no idea what to expect.

A SMALL LOG HOUSE APPEARED.

MR. COOK HUNTED ANIMALS.

2

At her new home, Minty was expected to help the young married mistress, Mrs. Cook, with her work as a weaver. She worked at home on a spinning wheel and loom, while Mr. Cook trapped fish and hunted animals for a living. The Cooks owned very little land and were not at all wealthy, but their log house was still the biggest one Minty had ever been in. She'd never set foot in the Big House on the Brodases' plantation when she had lived with her parents.

Though the Cooks' house had more than one

room, Minty was expected to sleep on the floor next to the kitchen fireplace, as if she were a dog. They fed her about as much as they'd feed a dog, too. The Cooks wanted a willing and productive worker, but they were unwilling to spend even one cent more than it took to just barely keep their new slave alive.

Minty's job was to wind yarn while Mrs. Cook worked the wheel and loom. Yarn fuzz constantly got in Minty's nose and mouth, making her sneeze or cough. As hard as she tried, she couldn't perform her task properly, and she hated every minute of it. She was afraid of the Cooks because of their cruelty. Constant hunger pains dominated her waking hours, and she slept fitfully on the cold, hard floor. Most of all, she was homesick. Mrs. Cook scolded Minty constantly but never lifted a finger to improve her living conditions. Naturally Minty's work continued to be clumsy and slow. Finally Mrs. Cook handed Minty over to Mr. Cook. "See if she's any help to you outside. She's no use to me."

Mr. Cook showed Minty how to tend the muskrat

MRS. COOK WORKED THE LOOM.

traps in the river while he hunted elsewhere. The animals were highly valued for their fur. Minty moved back and forth, watching the line of baskets in the cold water. When she found a trapped muskrat, it took all her young strength to haul it out of the river. Some days it was so cold, she could hardly feel her bare feet.

In spite of the cold, Minty was relieved to be out of the house and off by herself. She'd learned to appreciate God's natural world from Poppa.

Although Poppa had never been allowed to learn to read, he was the smartest man Minty knew. He could predict the weather for the next day or the next season simply by watching the sky or observing animals in the woods. He knew which herbs and plants were poisonous and which were useful for healing. He understood how the phases of the moon could be used as a guide for successful farming or fishing. He was familiar with the shapes of all the constellations in the night sky, and he showed his daughter how they moved with the seasons.

MINTY WATCHED THE BASKETS IN THE WATER.

In particular, he pointed out the North Star. It held a special meaning for Poppa and all other slaves, though it was seldom spoken of openly. As the long days and hungry nights dragged on, Minty began to understand his passion for that one stationary point of light: The North Star led to freedom.

In the half-light, just before dawn, Minty would often look for the North Star and think of Momma and Poppa. She knew they were trapped just like those river muskrats. As Minty prayed for a change in all their lives, a dream of freedom grew in the secret places of her soul.

The first step down the road toward her dream almost killed her. Minty came down with the measles. At the time when she lived, many illnesses could kill a child, but measles was one of the deadliest.

In spite of Minty's fever and weakness, the Cooks insisted that she continue wading barefoot in the cold river to haul in the heavy baskets with their trapped muskrats.

The fever increased, and Minty developed severe

POPPA POINTED OUT THE NORTH STAR.

bronchitis. She grew weaker, and every breath was painful. One day she simply collapsed. The Cooks wrapped her in a blanket and left her alone.

Among the slaves who worked on the great plantations and even among those who worked for less wealthy owners, an amazing network of personal communication existed. All the white masters understood that the slaves knew more about what was going on in the Big House, and knew it sooner, than the white folks who lived there did. And news about the slaves themselves always traveled rapidly from one place to another. Word about Minty's serious illness was quickly relayed to the Brodas plantation.

Momma Ross went to Master Brodas and begged to have her child back. "That child's gonna die if I don't nurse her back to health myself," Momma insisted.

Master Brodas was moved by her plea and sent for Mr. Cook and Minty. "Let her people make her well," he told Mr. Cook. "I don't know how they do

THE COOKS WRAPPED HER IN A BLANKET.

it, but they usually succeed. Then I'll send her back to you."

Mr. Cook was relieved. If Minty died, he would lose his investment, and he didn't want that. He agreed wholeheartedly to the plan and went home, leaving Minty behind.

Minty was carried back to her momma's cabin. With the help of potions homemade from the herbs Poppa gathered in the woods, she slowly regained her health. Momma made Minty eat until she couldn't hold anymore. It was clear the Cooks weren't feeding her much. Finally she was healthy enough to return to the Cooks' house.

However, the effects of severe bronchitis at such a young age forever altered Minty's voice. It became deep and husky, not like a child's at all. For the rest of her life, people could identify her by the distinct sound of her voice shouting out the cadences of a work song, praising Jesus in worship, or whispering words of freedom in the night.

Back at the Cooks', things were as bad as

MINTY SLOWLY REGAINED HER HEALTH.

before—even worse since Minty was now seen as too weak to work outdoors. Once again she took up weaving work, though she still had no heart for it and was just as clumsy as before. Finally the Cooks gave up on her and took her back to Brodas. They claimed she was stupid and lazy.

"We aren't about to keep feeding someone who won't work," Mrs. Cook insisted, her voice full of self-righteous scorn.

Minty was happy to be back living with her parents in their small cabin in the slave quarters on the Brodas plantation. Though she was now only seven and considered sickly, she was still expected to work. All slaves worked from the time they were old enough to leave their mothers. Even the littlest ones carried water to the field hands.

Momma and Poppa Ross were worried that Minty had become too much of a problem for the master and that he might sell her off. He'd done it before with two of their small daughters. The Rosses didn't think they could bear that again, especially

THE LITTLEST ONES CARRIED WATER.

with their youngest and smartest child, Minty.

But times were ripe for another big slave sale on the plantation. To keep up his standard of living, Mr. Brodas needed cash. When the crops weren't good—and they hadn't been lately—he sold timber from his forest. And slaves.

More and more plantations were supporting themselves by breeding, raising, and selling slaves, as if the slaves were nothing more than horses. And the chain gangs kept stopping by, looking for new slaves to replace the ones they had killed through neglect and overwork. The community of people living in the slave quarters was constantly threatened with the loss of relatives and friends.

Fortunately, little Minty wasn't snapped up by a chain gang, but Master Brodas did sell her once more. This time she went to a relatively prosperous family living in another Big House.

Her new mistress was called Miss Susan, and Minty, still a little girl, was to take care of Miss Susan's only child. Minty was so small for her age

THE CHAIN GANGS WERE
LOOKING FOR NEW SLAVES.

that she couldn't hold the baby properly while sitting or standing, so she would sit on the floor and hold the child in her lap. Minty became a living cradle for the baby. And the child stayed in Minty's lap all day unless Miss Susan was feeding him.

At night, when the baby slept in a real cradle, Minty slept on the floor nearby. Or rather, didn't sleep. She was expected to rock the cradle any time the baby cried and help him get back to sleep. And this was an especially fussy baby. Minty soon learned how to drift in and out of sleep while rocking the cradle constantly.

Minty was also expected to help Miss Susan keep the house clean and care for the furniture. This quickly became a nightmare.

Minty had never lived anywhere but in log cabins. She had never even seen anything like the polished furniture, carved wood, and carpets that filled the many rooms in this Big House. Minty had grown up playing on a dirt floor in her parents' cabin. Even at the Cooks', she had slept next to

SHE ROCKED THE CRADLE
ANY TIME THE BABY CRIED.

ashes in the fireplace. When Miss Susan told her to dust, Minty had no idea what that meant.

Her life had always included a little dirt, dust, and ash. Poppa used to say, "We all eat a bushel of dirt 'fore we die." The life-giving earth and the warming fire were friends to be accepted, not enemies to be fought. Why would anyone try to remove all trace of them?

Minty had no idea how to care for this woman's house. She didn't even know what questions to ask. From the very beginning, she was terrified of making mistakes, just as she had been at the Cooks'.

Miss Susan made a difficult situation impossible because she was neither patient nor kind. Rather than trying to help Minty by explaining how things were done, she reacted to Minty's lack of knowledge by calling her stupid. When harsh words brought no changes, she quickly brought out a whip and began whipping Minty. Fortunately, Miss Susan's sister intervened, severely scolding her sister for whipping a child. Then the sister carefully

SHE BROUGHT OUT A WHIP.

taught Minty how to clean a house.

Even after her sister's tongue-lashing, Miss Susan still enjoyed using that whip. If the baby cried, she whipped Minty. If the house wasn't kept spotless, she whipped Minty.

One day, Miss Susan caught Minty "stealing" a lump of sugar from the sugar bowl. Out came the whip, but this time Minty ran. She had already taken as much abuse as she could stand. She ran crying through the house, pushing startled servants and family members aside. Out the front door she rushed and sprinted for the nearby woods, trying to find a place to hide from her tormentor. Miss Susan and her husband chased her for a little ways, but finally gave up.

Minty stayed in hiding until hunger and thirst began to eat away at her. For several days, she hid in a pigpen, fighting with the pigs for food and water. Even though she loved the outdoors, she had no idea how to survive on her own. She had never learned enough about the lay of the land to find her way back

SHE HID IN A PIGPEN.

to the Brodas plantation and seek shelter with her momma and poppa.

Eventually she came out of hiding and dragged herself back to her mistress. Minty was hungry, filthy, and frightened that Miss Susan might kill her. Miss Susan almost did.

This whipping was the most severe Minty had ever received. When Miss Susan had worn herself out from screaming and beating the child with the short rawhide whip, she left Minty lying on the ground near the back of the house, bleeding from deep tears on her back and nearly unconscious from pain. Then she went to fetch her husband. Together, they decided to take her back to Master Brodas and ask for their money back. They had the same complaints as the Cooks—that Minty was stupid and lazy.

Master Brodas turned Minty over to her momma again, this time to heal the bleeding whip marks that crisscrossed numerous older scars.

Momma had seldom been as angry with the

THIS WHIPPING WAS THE MOST SEVERE.

white folks as she was now. Even so, she only spoke of it within the relative safety of the cabin walls. Sometimes she talked to Poppa about it, but usually she just cried out to the Lord. "Whipping a child like this. Don't feed her, don't clean her up, and then they *whip* her like a dog."

While she talked, Momma sponged cool, herbal teas onto Minty's back and neck. "What's gonna come of my baby, dear Jesus?" she asked in an anguished voice. "Lord, make her strong. Protect this child. Work Your mysterious ways in her life." Then she softly sang and cried.

Minty slept soundly on her stomach for days, letting her wounds heal and making up for all that sleep she'd lost rocking the white baby's cradle and fighting with hungry pigs. Momma's comforting voice floated through Minty's dreams, and she knew, even asleep, that she was safe. When she was awake, Momma fed her cornbread and rich goat's milk to fatten her up a little and give her strength.

While Minty was getting her health back,

"LORD, PROTECT THIS CHILD."

Master Brodas let Momma know that he wasn't going to sell Minty again. This time, he wanted to hire her out. This would allow her to continue living at the plantation while she worked for someone nearby. Momma was glad Minty would be staying with them, but she was worried about how she would do in her new job. She had hoped Minty could learn a useful indoor trade so that she could live an easier life as a household slave. Master Brodas wanted to hire her out as a field hand, even though she was not yet ten years old.

"What You got in mind, Lord?" Momma prayed. "You better help her hold up in that hot sun, Lord. Teach her how to earn her keep. Please don't let her go away on the chain gang."

Then she rocked and moaned as her Minty slept next to her, safe and sound—for that day at least.

MASTER BRODAS WANTED TO HIRE HER OUT.

MINTY TRIED TO REASON WITH A MULE.

3

The sun beat down mercilessly as Minty tried to reason with a mule. Years had passed, and she was now a valued field hand. Her instinctive knowledge of animals and her love for all things in the outdoors were unique skills that gave her a special status, even as a slave.

Her skinny frame had filled out, giving her the lean muscular body of a strong young woman. Her arms, legs, and shoulders had hardened like a man's. Though she never grew over five feet tall, her back was straight and strong. Her bare feet and her hard-working hands were protected by layers of tough calluses.

Minty had long since stopped wearing a child's sack garment. Now she wore a woman's dress, which she managed to twist into something like trousers when necessary in the field. She also wore a colorful bandanna tied around her head, like the other grown women.

Minty was expected to lift, pick, push, and plow like a man. And she rose to the occasion because she loved to be outdoors. Even while she was working, there was time to study the landscape, the birds, and the river. Her deep, husky voice often joined those of her fellow workers in songs that would rise up out of the fields and soar above the trees, straight on up to Jesus.

Every day of breathing fresh air instead of wool lint or soiled diapers made Minty grateful to God. The Lord did indeed work in mysterious ways. What Momma had thought was all wrong on the master's part had actually been right for Minty. The

MINTY WAS EXPECTED TO WORK LIKE A MAN.

Lord's hand had brought her to this work, she knew.

She began to sing a song written by a man who spent years kidnaping and selling slaves until the day when Jesus showed him what a terrible thing he was doing. People said the man never sold another slave. Sometimes, Minty wondered what kinds of changes God had in store for her life.

Amazing grace, how sweet the sound
That saved a wretch like me...

The rest of the field hands joined her:

I once was lost but now am found,
Was blind but now I see.

After several verses the song died away. Sometimes, singing was the only thing that made their hard work bearable. But today, as Minty tried reasoning with the mule, her song was one of simple praise to God.

SINGING MADE THEIR HARD WORK BEARABLE.

HARRIET TUBMAN

A new song started up, and a field hand walked up behind Minty. "You hear about Joe Dubois?" he said softly, counting on the sound of the music to hide his words from the ever-watchful white overseers.

Minty shook her head. She knew Joe, a dark-skinned, gentle giant of a man.

"He heard he was going to the chain gang for big money, and he ran." He pulled at a leather strap on the mule's harness, pretending to adjust it. "He got on that Underground Railroad, sister. He ain't never gonna work these fields again, praise the Lord." Then he quietly walked away.

Minty kept her hands moving along the mule's harness, but her mind was no longer on the adjustments she needed to make. What was the field hand talking about? She'd seen plenty of trains. Trains were used by white folks, and a few blacks as well, to travel long distances. At night she could hear their sad whistles from miles away.

But a train under the ground?

"HE GOT ON THAT UNDERGROUND RAILROAD, SISTER."

It took some time and a lot of whispered questions at night in various slave cabins, but eventually Minty understood the Underground Railroad.

To begin with, it was not a railroad, nor did it run through some big tunnel under the ground. There were white folks who didn't believe in slavery, people who felt the same way about it as the man who wrote the hymn "Amazing Grace." Mostly they lived up North, but some could be found in the South.

These people believed that the living Christ had called them to free all the slaves. Many were Quakers, who wore odd clothing and talked like characters out of some Bible story, using words like "thee" and "thou" when speaking to their friends. Others were Methodists, who were always trying to figure out how God wanted them to act in the smallest details of their daily lives.

All of them believed without a doubt that the Lord had made all humans equal. They also believed that the Constitution of the United States had been written to protect that equality. They were willing to

THE QUAKERS BELIEVED THAT
THE LORD HAD MADE ALL HUMANS EQUAL.

risk their lives to fight the evil of slavery by helping slaves escape to freedom in the North.

Minty had never heard of such white people. She certainly had never known any like that. Miss Susan's sister had shown her a little compassion, and that was surprising in itself. But could it be true that some white folks actually wanted to free *all* the slaves?

As she carefully questioned other slaves in the fields, she discovered there were many routes that led to the North and freedom. Even slaves in the Deep South could find routes that took them to boats and across the Caribbean Sea.

In Maryland and most other parts of the South, escaping slaves traveled mainly on foot. There were special code words everyone used to describe the system. A "station" was a house that would provide food, shelter, and money. Runaway slaves were called "passengers," and those who guided them along the routes were called "conductors." Once the runaways reached the northern states, many committed people, both free blacks and whites, would help them start a new life of

ESCAPING SLAVES TRAVELED MAINLY ON FOOT.

freedom in this strange new land.

This all sounded like a magical train bound for heaven to Minty, but everyone insisted the Underground Railroad truly existed. You simply had to know the right white person and have the courage to leave your master.

Know white people? Minty thought when she heard this. *And trust white people?* She shook her head. How could she trust people who treated her like an animal, who believed they had the right to own her? That was just plain foolish.

One day, a short time later, Minty was squatting down picking strawberries in the south fields. The sun wasn't so brutally hot, and the berries were coming off the vine as easy as could be. As she dragged her berry basket down the row, Minty thought back over everything she'd heard about the Underground Railroad, with its stations and conductors.

Trust Me.

Minty looked up. Who said that? She straightened her back and looked around. It had been a

HOW COULD SHE TRUST WHITE PEOPLE?

mature voice, a deep male voice. But there were only women picking nearby, and the overseer was on the far side of the field.

Sometimes, so the old folks said, the hot sun could make people hear or see strange things in the fields. That was why they encouraged new field hands to wear a straw hat in the midday sun. Minty thought about that. She was no newcomer, and there wasn't enough sun to get excited over. She frowned and bent over the next plant.

Trust Me.

Now she stood up, then quickly squatted back down before the overseer noticed. She began to tremble. "Oh Lord," she whispered. "You talking to me?"

There was silence. She kept picking strawberries automatically, but her mind grappled wildly with the words she knew she'd heard. The hair on her neck stood up in the same way it did when the hymns in the slave quarters on Sunday were particularly powerful. Could this be the Lord's doing?

"I have always trusted You, Lord," she prayed

"OH LORD," SHE WHISPERED.
"YOU TALKING TO ME?"

softly, moving to the next plant.

Trust Me.

Three times. Even though she could not read, Minty knew enough about the Bible to realize that a command spoken three times was meant to be taken seriously. This was surely a message from God for her to think on and figure out.

She nodded and silently finished her work. If God was going to act on her behalf, if He was asking her to trust His ability to intervene directly in her life, then perhaps her mistrust of white people would make no difference.

"I hear You, Lord," she prayed quietly. "I will trust You to show me the way out of here and the proper time to leave."

By the time she was twelve years old, Minty was as strong as any man on the plantation. She was also short and slim and female, so that neither Master Brodas nor his overseers felt the least bit threatened by her.

MINTY WAS AS STRONG AS ANY MAN.

Because of her hard work, outward obedience, and lack of chatter, Master Brodas considered Minty a good slave. Many times when her husky, full-voiced singing set the pace for work in the fields, he congratulated himself on his decision to keep her working for his plantation.

But Master Brodas had no idea of the revolution that had taken place in Minty's mind. She was convinced that slavery was wrong, and she was determined to find a way to freedom for herself and all of her people. She was only waiting on the Lord to show her the right time to act.

That fall, during the part of the harvest when the corn was shucked, Minty noticed a slave acting oddly. She glanced around, still stripping the outer leaves off the husks, to see if anyone else noticed. He was shucking very slowly and seemed nervous, even jumpy. That was no way to act around an overseer. Fortunately, the overseer had his back turned to the slave.

Suddenly the slave broke away from the crowd

HE WAS SHUCKING VERY SLOWLY AND SEEMED NERVOUS.

of workers and ran. He was halfway across the field before the overseer noticed and took off after him, whip in hand.

Usually overseers did their work mounted. The horse allowed them to intimidate the workers and also to move quickly. But this overseer had been inspecting the harvest on foot, and he was so angry that he hadn't taken the time to go after his horse on the other side of the field. Even so, he was rapidly gaining ground on the fleeing slave.

Minty was terribly frightened for the runaway. Without thinking, she took off after the overseer. She found both men in a dim storage building just beyond the cornfield. The overseer wanted to whip the slave immediately, and when he saw Minty, he ordered her to tie the man to one of the large wooden posts that held up the building's roof. Minty simply stood there and looked at the two men.

Suddenly the slave darted past her and ran toward the open door. The overseer moved to follow, but Minty blocked his way. The overseer was surprised

MINTY BLOCKED HIS WAY.

and frustrated. He wanted to stop the fleeing slave, so he grabbed a two-pound brick and threw it after the man.

The throw was much too short, and the brick hit Minty square in the forehead, knocking her out. She collapsed to the dusty floor with a sickening thud, and a rapidly growing pool of blood appeared around her head.

The slave got away, but Minty's life would never be the same.

SHE COLLAPSED TO THE DUSTY FLOOR.

MOMMA ROSS WORRIED AND PRAYED.

4

Once again, Minty lay on a pallet in her momma's cabin. This time she was unconscious most of the time. It was obvious to everyone that she was near death. The brick had cracked her skull, and there was an ugly, frightening hole in her forehead. She slept and slept.

Even during those parts of the day when she appeared to be awake, she had actually dozed off. For months Momma Ross worked on her daughter's wound, dressing it with herbs while she worried and prayed over her semiconscious child.

Word of Minty's brave and selfless act that helped a slave escape spread quickly. Because of their admiration for her, the slave community changed her name. They would no longer use her baby name. From now on, she would be called by her mother's name, Harriet. This was a tremendous honor. It was a way people in the quarters could show their respect for one of their own without actually speaking about her act of outright rebellion.

Now there were two questions on everyone's lips. Would young Harriet survive, and what would the master do with her if she did? It didn't look like she'd ever pull out of the stupor she was in, much less return to being the hearty young woman she'd been before her injury.

Momma Ross prayed hard. "Lord, I know You can pull my baby through. And I know You make good from evil. Let Harriet live, and use her life for Your purposes."

November passed, then Christmas. Harriet was still unable to speak or walk. Winter came and went.

HARRIET WAS UNABLE TO SPEAK OR WALK.

Finally, as spring approached and the natural world woke up from its long sleep, so did Harriet. The wound was now a nasty scar. She was actually able to remain conscious for the entire day, though she stayed quiet for several more weeks. Miraculously, Harriet had been given a new life to go with her new name. Her parents thanked the Lord.

When Master Brodas heard Harriet was recovering, he tried to sell her, but prospective buyers just laughed. All they could see was a slave who was physically weak, obviously rebellious, and because of the scar on her forehead, frightening to look at. Although Harriet was on the mend, she still had horrible headaches. The scar itself was painful, and she was prone to fainting spells. She never knew when she would fall into a deep sleep. She had no control over it at all. She could be standing on the dirt path in front of her parents' cabin or in the middle of a conversation with a friend, and she would simply collapse on the ground, sound asleep. When this happened, no one could wake her up.

SHE WAS PRONE TO FAINTING SPELLS.

During these periods of deep unconsciousness, she would sometimes have detailed visions full of vivid images. As Harriet floated in and out of touch with life in the slave quarters, these visions often seemed more real than her actual surroundings.

With her body slowly healing, she had a lot of time to think about what had happened to her. She was sure that she had been spared—and even changed—for a reason.

At first she believed God wanted her to pray for Master Brodas. She spent days in prayer, asking God to work on her white master and convert him. She maintained this pattern of nearly continuous prayer for weeks as she lay quietly on her pallet.

Having spent so many hours praying for her master's welfare, it came as a great shock to her when she learned that he was making arrangements to sell her, along with two of her brothers, to a chain gang. Harriet was truly frightened. She was still too weak to survive the terrible conditions the slaves working on chain gangs had to endure. She was

SHE SPENT DAYS IN PRAYER.

even too sick to run away.

Her fear quickly became a dark anger that turned all her thoughts ugly and vengeful. She began praying that God would kill Master Brodas. When her headaches tormented her, these prayers became a steady chanting inside her throbbing head: *Kill him, Lord. Kill him.* She was totally obsessed with the idea of punishing this white man who had done so many evil things to her and her family.

A few days later, Edward Brodas suddenly became ill, and a few days after that, he died.

As soon as Harriet learned of her master's death, she was horrified and guilt-stricken. Though she desperately wanted to believe otherwise, she was sure that her prayers had killed Master Brodas.

A severe headache seized her, and she collapsed onto her pallet in the cabin, curling into a shaking ball of pain. With what little strength she had left, she begged God for forgiveness and asked for opportunities to do good in the world around her.

One day she would understand that Master

EDWARD BRODAS BECAME ILL AND DIED.

Brodas had not died because of her prayers, but for now she was filled with remorse. Though Harriet firmly believed in the power of prayer for the rest of her long life, she could never again bring herself to pray that anything evil should happen to another human being.

The death of Edward Brodas was followed by a time of confusion and mourning. There was no way to anticipate what his heir would do with the plantation and its slaves. Sometimes a change of ownership meant that all the slaves were sold, often breaking up families.

As the slaves on the Brodas plantation sang their long, slow songs of mourning far into the night, they were expressing their own worries for the future as well as paying their respects to their master's memory.

Fortunately, the heir was a doctor and minister who decided to leave the plantation and its work force largely undisturbed. In the future, if slaves had to be sold, they would only go to owners living in

THE SLAVES SANG SONGS OF MOURNING.

the state of Maryland. Everyone in the quarters breathed a little easier.

In time, Harriet recovered enough of her strength to perform household tasks and was hired out to a man named Stewart. After a short while, she insisted that she was feeling much better and appealed to Stewart for more outside work. Stewart agreed to let her be a field hand again and soon discovered that Harriet could do just as much work as any man. However, because she was a woman, Stewart didn't have to pay as much for her labor.

The hard work in the fields made Harriet even stronger than she had been before her injury. She grew so strong that Master Stewart would invite his friends over to watch her lift and throw heavy items. Later he developed a surprise ending for his demonstrations. Harriet would put on a special harness and tow a barge down the river while walking along the bank. His friends loved the show, but Harriet felt like an animal doing tricks.

Master Stewart was so pleased with Harriet that

HARRIET COULD TOW A BARGE DOWN THE RIVER.

he allowed her free time to hire herself out. The money she made was hers to keep. Harriet also had numerous opportunities to help her poppa cut timber in the woods. She gained a whole new appreciation for this quietly wise man.

He picked right up where he had left off years ago and continued teaching his daughter everything he knew about nature. Harriet sensed a new urgency in his lessons. Poppa Ross knew his daughter was too special not to be free, and he wanted to give her the knowledge she would need to escape someday. Though they never spoke of this openly, Harriet came to understand his real goal.

Poppa showed Harriet which herbs were valuable as medicines and explained how to use them in healing. He pointed out the roots and berries that were edible and warned her about those that were dangerous.

He taught her as much as he knew about the geography of Maryland—information about rivers, marshes, and forests, as well as the locations of

HARRIET HELPED HER POPPA CUT TIMBER.

major roads and towns. She soon realized that he had learned a great deal on his many trips away from the plantation with Master Brodas.

Poppa showed Harriet how to find her way through the darkest forest at night using the stars as a compass. And he reminded her that the North Star still pointed the way to freedom.

Most important, Poppa Ross taught Harriet how to move quietly in the woods. "A forest is a noisy thing when you listen to it," Poppa explained. The perfect beauty of God's world had been stained by human rebellion in the Garden of Eden. Poppa believed that one result of that tragedy was the unnecessary noise that constantly disturbed the peace of the natural world.

Harriet learned to listen for twigs breaking, birds chirping, owls hooting, deer scampering, rabbits scurrying, and branches crashing to the forest floor. Poppa taught her not only how to listen to sounds and interpret them, but also how to mimic hoot owls and other birds.

POPPA TAUGHT HER HOW TO MIMIC HOOT OWLS.

Finally he helped her to listen for the noises she made in the woods, and then he showed her how to eliminate them. Soon she could glide through the trees like a shadow. She even managed to creep up on her old father and startle him a few times. Each time he was pleased with her, very pleased, and a hopeful light began to grow in his eyes.

Life went on without any serious problems for several years in the Ross family. Harriet continued to work hard and hire herself out for some money of her own.

But as she moved into her twenties, Harriet found that something in her life was missing. She found herself listening to the mourning doves and their plaintive songs.

"Mourning dove crying for rain," Momma had always told her. But the field hands said, "Mourning dove crying for its mate."

A mate. A husband. That's what was missing. Harriet was aware of soft new feelings—a desire to

SHE FOUND HERSELF LISTENING TO THE MOURNING DOVES.

marry a good man, maybe have children. For the first time, she shyly observed the men around her in a different light. She wondered who might make a suitable husband.

When a man called John Tubman noticed Harriet, she knew her quest for love was finished. Serious young Harriet found a balance to her somber personality in this handsome, laughing man. Maybe the fact that John was a free man made him that much more appealing. At any rate, Harriet fell in love.

Slaves didn't have weddings or legal marriages in the manner of white folks. But slaves did have a marriage ceremony called "jumping the broom." Slaves who wished to marry asked permission of the master, and if he agreed to the union, the betrothed and their families would gather around a broom lying on the floor. Then the couple would jump together over the broom. This symbolized their commitment to each other. Sometimes, if the master was a more devout Christian man, he would

THE COUPLE WOULD JUMP TOGETHER OVER THE BROOM.

make certain there was a religious ceremony for the new couple.

In 1844, John Tubman and Harriet Ross were married, making a commitment to spend the rest of their lives together. Harriet left her parents' cabin and moved in with her new husband.

IN 1844, JOHN TUBMAN AND HARRIET ROSS WERE MARRIED.

THE CROSSWHITES TRAVELED SECRETLY.

5

In 1846, a family of slaves by the name of Cross-white traveled secretly from Kentucky to a way station on the Underground Railroad in the small northern town of Marshall, Michigan. That part of Michigan was being settled mostly by New Yorkers who left everything behind them and had traveled down the Erie Canal looking for good farmland.

These New Yorkers brought with them a deep hatred of slavery. Because of this, Michigan became a final destination for many slaves from Kentucky and other nearby slave states. The Crosswhite family, like many fugitive families, was grateful for the hospitality of the citizens of Marshall and decided to settle there.

One day slavers from Kentucky appeared and demanded to take the Crosswhite family back to the plantation from which they had escaped. But the leaders of Marshall had the constables arrest the slavers on the charge of kidnaping and throw them in jail.

By the time the Kentuckians were released, the Crosswhite family had been spirited across Michigan and were on their way to Canada.

This was one of countless stories of heroism that encouraged slaves in their quest for freedom. It was also one of many incidents that would eventually cause Congress to draft and pass the Fugitive Slave Law in 1850, which would say that runaway slaves could be returned to the South and made it a crime to help runaways even in the free soil of the North.

Harriet always listened for any encouraging tidbits of news regarding runaway slaves. John Tubman was free because his parents had been freed after

THE CONSTABLES ARRESTED THE SLAVERS.

their master's death. But she, his wife, was a slave. Her entire family were slaves. She could be sold whether or not her husband was free, and if that happened, she might never see John or any of her family members again.

One night she told John about the Crosswhites in Michigan. Her eyes were alight with excitement, though she kept her voice low. She began to speak to him about running away together.

John Tubman, usually good-natured, became very agitated. He had his freedom already, and he did not think it necessary for Harriet to be free. Most of all, he did not want her to do anything that would jeopardize their fairly comfortable way of life.

This shocked Harriet. "But John," she said, "you're a free man. Don't you want that for me? Don't you want children someday and have them be free?"

"We're all right just the way we are," John declared angrily. "I make my own money, and you're able to hire out for money, too. We got our own place.

"YOU'RE A FREE MAN."

We aren't so bad off."

But things weren't all that good, either. Times were hard on the plantation. Cotton prices were going down, and everyone knew what that meant—more slaves would be sold to the chain gang. Harriet was terrified it would happen to her.

She appealed to her husband again. "Please, John," she whispered, "I know we can do this. Slaves go north all the time. There's a way. Then nobody would ever be able to separate us!" John Tubman simply shook his head.

Harriet started having a series of dreams at night. In them, she could see and hear the terrors of slaves being rousted out of their cabins at night and sold. She could see and hear the chain gang trudging, their irons clanking, the slaves weeping. Then she dreamed she was swimming across a river. Just as she was about to go down in the deep water and drown, women dressed in white reached out, grabbed her flailing arms, and pulled her across.

She decided the first dream was a warning from

MORE SLAVES WOULD BE SOLD TO THE CHAIN GANG.

God that she was going to be sold, and the second dream was a comfort from God that she should head north and His angels would watch over her. She decided to approach John again about running away by telling him about the dreams.

First he laughed at her. Then he became angry again. "Put this running away out of your head, Harriet."

"But John, they gonna sell me someday. You and me will never see each other again."

John Tubman did not respond to that. He simply bent down and put his face close to hers. It almost seemed like he was growling. "If you run, I'll tell the master."

Harriet stepped back. "You would tell on your own wife?"

"I'd tell him as fast as I could." John pounded his fist in his hand. Then he folded his arms and glared down at her.

"You know what they do to runaways," Harriet whispered. "You would let them do that to me?"

JOHN POUNDED HIS FIST IN HIS HAND.

"Try running and see," he said. She looked deep into his eyes and saw no love there. For the first time, Harriet was afraid of John.

Harriet was terribly hurt to discover that her own husband would betray her to the master. Yet John Tubman was the only man Harriet had ever loved, and even the hurt he caused her could not kill her love for him.

But she knew the Lord wanted to help her be free, always had known it. She was also certain that the time would come when he would see it her way. Then she would come back for him. But that time was not now. Harriet became even more determined to leave. She not only watched for the right time to escape, but she also watched John closely so that he would not know of her plans. She did not doubt for a minute that he would turn on her.

By 1849, three years after the Crosswhite affair in Michigan, enough time had elapsed without Harriet leaving that John Tubman no longer seemed suspicious. Harriet noted it and was relieved. But it

"TRY RUNNING AND SEE!"

wasn't yet time to leave.

One day a white woman approached Harriet while she was working in the fields near the road. Harriet had never looked at white people's faces much. In the South, blacks did not look whites in the eyes, and Harriet found their faces frightening anyway. They seemed to have no insides, no warmth.

But she found herself looking directly at the white woman. She was old and had the kindest face Harriet had seen except for her own mother's. This old woman had straight, thin white hair parted neatly in the center, eyes as gray as a spring rain cloud, and soft-looking skin with blue veins showing at her temples. She wore a simple dress and bonnet, the attire of a farmer's wife. She was very clean and crisp.

The old woman had reined in her horse and turned in her wagon to face Harriet. She smiled, looking right into Harriet's eyes, and began chatting about the day, the weather, the crops. The woman

SHE WORE A SIMPLE DRESS AND BONNET.

was friendly and talkative, and for the first time in her life, Harriet found herself talking normally and naturally to someone who was not black. This woman seemed be a decent person.

Suddenly Harriet remembered God telling her in the strawberry field to trust Him. It had been years. What was going to happen? Did it have something to do with this white woman? For the time being, Harriet decided simply to get to know the woman better. They chatted a couple times each week at the side of the road.

Suddenly things started to change on the plantation. Slaves were being sold off. Before anyone knew what was happening, two of Harriet's sisters were gone on the chain gang. Her parents were mortified. Panic filled the slave quarters.

Harriet found herself sharing the news with her new white friend. The woman never hesitated. She quietly said, "If you ever need anything, Harriet—anything at all—you know where I live. You hear me?"

SLAVES WERE BEING SOLD OFF.

Harriet nodded, and the old woman rode off on her wagon. Maybe, Harriet thought, the women dressed in white in the dreams represented white women instead of angels.

The time had come, Harriet decided, to run for it. But she was afraid to go alone. She didn't dare tell John, but she did ask three of her brothers to go with her. They agreed, and plans were made.

On the night of their escape, Harriet waited until John was asleep. Then she met her brothers near the fields. Off they went.

But after only a mile, her brothers' fears got the better of them. They decided to go back. Furthermore, they forced their baby sister to return with them.

Harriet was angry with her brothers, and she realized that if she was going to escape, she'd have to do it alone. She'd just have to wait for the right time. She slipped back into her cabin. Fortunately John was sound asleep and hadn't noticed she'd left.

The right time came two days later when a field hand told Harriet that he'd just learned the chain

SHE MET HER BROTHERS NEAR THE FIELDS.

gang was taking Harriet and her three brothers that very night. Now she knew she'd have to leave as soon as it was dark.

There was plenty about the upcoming journey to frighten Harriet. The lack of food and shelter, the fact that she'd never traveled anywhere alone before, the need to travel only at night and stay hidden during the day, the threat of being hunted down by bloodhounds and returned to be whipped—all these were good reasons to be afraid.

But it was also her own body that Harriet had to consider. She was afraid it would betray her. Her scar made her easily recognizable. She had an unusually lean yet muscular build for a woman, and nobody who ever heard her deep voice could forget it. Her headaches and blackouts could come at any time. She might be crossing a road in full view of anyone and fall into a deep sleep. Or she could be crossing a river and drown because of a blackout.

In the middle of her panic, Harriet felt the assurance of the Lord settle over her. She believed this

SHE WAS AFRAID.

journey was blessed. She would trust in the Lord. He would see her through.

That night Harriet rose in the dark and tied some food up in a kerchief. Then she left the cabin and John Tubman. It hurt to leave the only man she'd ever loved, even if he didn't love her as much as she'd hoped he did. But she also felt she had no choice. She simply could not be sold to a chain gang, never to see any of her loved ones again.

She left the plantation by way of the back of the Big House where Harriet's sister was a cook. Because of the hot weather and the heat of cooking, the kitchen on a plantation was in a separate building a few steps from the Big House. Staying well outside the kitchen where her sister was working, Harriet composed a song on the spot and sang it so the sister would know where she'd be:

Good-bye, I'm going to leave you,
Good-bye, I'll meet you in the Kingdom. . . .

SHE LEFT THE CABIN.

HARRIET TUBMAN

And so Harriet set out for freedom. Her first stop was the old white woman's house. The woman didn't seem the least bit surprised to see Harriet. She sat Harriet down and explained the Underground Railroad more fully to her, then she wrote two names on a piece of paper.

"These are the next places for you to stop," she said. "You'll be safe there. I'll tell you how to get to the first one, and you show them this paper. They'll tell you how to get to the next stop. There will be many stops like these where people will feed you and shelter you and direct you. Soon enough you'll be in Philadelphia."

Harriet felt a bit rattled, but when the kind old woman offered to pray over her, she calmed down. She remembered the dreams and the words of the Lord: *Trust Me*.

Finally she said good-bye to the first white person she would call friend, and Harriet Tubman headed for the woods, following the North Star.

"SHOW THEM THIS PAPER."

SHE USED HER KNOWLEDGE OF THE WOODS.

6

Harriet's destination was Philadelphia, Pennsylvania, where there was a network of freed slaves and other concerned people to help her start a new life. Fortunately Maryland, where Harriet lived, was fairly close to Pennsylvania—about ninety miles. But she would still have to travel many miles on foot during several days and nights of uncertainty and fear.

Harriet left the old woman's house in the dark of night, and she used all her knowledge of the woods to get her through that dark forest. She kept moving all night, quickly, quickly. Every step was one more step away from the bloodhounds and the whip. With every step she prayed, "I trust You, Lord. . .I trust You, Lord." It became a hopeful rhythm for her as she moved through the trees and the underbrush.

And somehow by the end of that first night, Harriet lost her fear. She kept her wits about her, but her fear was gone, never to return in full measure. Years later, "fearless" was one of the words that everyone who knew Harriet would use to describe her.

The next morning she found the farmhouse the old woman had described. She handed her piece of paper to the woman who answered the kitchen door, and the woman smiled. "Come and eat," she said.

Harriet hadn't realized how hungry she was. She ate bacon and home-baked biscuits with blueberry preserves. The food was delicious, and it was a new experience for Harriet, a slave all her life, to be fed by a white woman. After breakfast, the woman

HARRIET HADN'T REALIZED HOW HUNGRY SHE WAS.

handed her a broom and suggested she sweep the yard. Folks in the South often had dirt yards that they would sweep into pretty patterns. Harriet had swept yards often in her childhood, and she did so now, happily. She realized that the law would never suspect a slave who was working out in the open of being a runaway.

She left the farm that night on the floor of the farmer's produce wagon, covered with a blanket and a load of fresh vegetables. She thought wistfully about her family and what would be happening back home. She dozed and dreamed and marveled that the Lord had taken away her fear.

The wagon stopped at a river in the dark hours of early morning. The farmer gave Harriet her next instructions and some advice. "Travel only at night. And don't set foot on the road, ever." Then he wished her Godspeed. Harriet thanked him and proceeded to follow the river northward.

Harriet walked all night to the next designated stop, this time on the riverbank. Here another stranger

HARRIET FOLLOWED THE RIVER NORTHWARD.

greeted her calmly and kindly, just as the first two white people had at their "stations." He helped her climb into his boat. He rowed for several miles, miles that Harriet would have had to walk had this good man not been part of a network of kind Christian folks.

At the end of their journey, he sent her on foot to another farm, where she was given a meal and a clever hiding spot inside a big round bale of hay that sat in the middle of a field full of such bales. Exhausted, she slept like a baby.

That night, the sky was overcast, and Harriet could not see the North Star. She was slowed down by this, but not stopped. She felt her way along in the dark from tree to tree, feeling for the damp moss that grows only on the north side and stumbling to the next tree. She managed to keep walking in the right direction.

Her next stop found her with a family of free blacks. For one entire week, they kept her in their cabin. She hid in a potato hole they had dug in their

FREE BLACKS KEPT HER IN THEIR CABIN.

cabin floor. Harriet was grateful for having grown up on dirt floors. She liked the smell of the earth, and she felt no fear down there. They fixed the same kinds of foods Momma would have made, and it felt nice.

When the way seemed clear again, the black family sent Harriet on her way. She continued to sleep on the ground by day and travel by night.

The next stop was a farm owned by German immigrants, people known as Pennsylvania Dutch. Harriet loved the tidy barns they'd painted black and the swept-out livestock corrals. Even the farm animals were clean! Harriet enjoyed listening to the Germans speak in their own language, too. They hid her in their attic and fed her rich food. It tasted different than anything Harriet had ever eaten, but it was delicious and wholesome.

Her next stop was Philadelphia and freedom. It had taken time to travel and hide. She'd been the grateful recipient of hospitality from more strangers than she'd ever met before! Not once had she had a

THEY FED HER RICH FOOD.

sleeping seizure, and she thanked God for that protection.

Now she was free! The thrill was indescribable. Her faith was strong. Not only had God seen her through, but He had shown her so many godly people in the world who were willing to risk their own lives for her. In spite of being far from home and family, Harriet's heart was lightened by such knowledge.

And Philadelphia was indeed a far cry from home. She'd never been in a city before, and Philadelphia was a big one. And it was cold! Harriet was a country woman, having grown up in a warm, humid part of the country listening to the soft sounds of birds and frogs and slave songs.

Now she heard horses clopping on the hard streets and people shouting all day long. Instead of smelling the sweetness in the damp air back home, here she smelled horse droppings and frying food. It didn't feel much like the Promised Land.

But it would do just fine. Harriet was free. She

HARRIET WAS FREE!

made herself adjust to the tall buildings and the fast, noisy way of life. She got jobs working in hotels and kitchens. She worked two and three jobs at a time, partly for the money, partly to stay busy.

And Harriet Tubman had a plan. She wanted to help other slaves. Running away had been dangerous, but it had been successful. Since arriving in Philadelphia, Harriet had met dozens of fugitive slaves. She came to know the organizations that helped them. She began to realize that to gain freedom, a slave needed courage, God's mercy, and the knowledge that it could be done.

Harriet also wanted her family with her. More importantly, she wanted every one of them to breathe freely, walk where they wished, and earn their own money. She wanted them to live with the amazing freedom she now had. If she could make it, they could, too! But they didn't know that. And they certainly didn't know how to go about it.

So Harriet determined that she would go back to Maryland as soon as she was able and spirit away

HARRIET HAD MET DOZENS OF FUGITIVE SLAVES.

her relatives. Maybe by now even John Tubman would change his mind and come with her. Her heart leaped at the thought.

One day someone from the Underground Railroad mentioned that a free black man needed help to get his wife and two small children, who were slaves, north. The volunteers who helped fugitives in Philadelphia wanted a woman to help, since one child was a baby. Harriet listened, then recognized the names of her sister Mary and her husband.

"They're about to be sold," the volunteers explained. "Your brother-in-law thinks they can escape, but Mary needs help with the little ones. Do you know of anyone?"

"Me," said Harriet. "I'll do it."

The volunteers were adamant that she not be the one. Harriet was a fugitive from Maryland with a bounty price on her head. There was no way she should return to the South.

But Harriet laughed them off. "I'm not afraid. I understand how the Underground Railroad works,

"I'M NOT AFRAID."

and I am the right person to bring them here."

And she was. A Quaker friend pretended to be a prospective slave buyer, and through a plan he had developed with Harriet's brave brother-in-law, Harriet's family was taken right off the slave auction block and hidden. They were able to escape to one station, on to another station, and then another.

Harriet waited for her family at a Quaker house in Baltimore. What a happy reunion! Then she confidently took them on the rest of the dangerous journey to Philadelphia.

One sister and that sister's family were now free and with Harriet. She made plans to get more kin and anyone else who truly wanted to be free.

Now Harriet knew why the Lord had spoken to her loud and clear. She decided to became a "conductor" for the Underground Railroad and devote her life to escorting slaves to freedom. That meant working and saving money for the journeys, staying close to the Fugitive Committee in Philadelphia, and eventually traveling to the South again.

A QUAKER FRIEND PRETENDED TO BE A SLAVE BUYER.

HARRIET TUBMAN

Traveling to southern states to bring more slaves to freedom was tremendously risky. It was just about the most dangerous thing Harriet could do. At any moment, she could be arrested as a fugitive slave. But Harriet knew God was on her side. And God made Harriet fearless.

GOD MADE HARRIET FEARLESS.

THE FUGITIVE SLAVE LAW WAS PASSED.

7

In 1850, one year after Harriet had escaped to freedom, the Fugitive Slave Law was passed by Congress. This new law did two things. It made it a crime to help runaways anywhere in America, and it allowed former masters to reclaim runaway slaves even in the free northern states.

Those slaves would then be returned to the South. This law agreed with southern slave owners that slaves were the legal property of their masters and that such property should be returned.

The men in Congress fought for a long time

over the Fugitive Slave Law. But in the end, they agreed to it, hoping it would prevent a war between the North and South.

Once passed, the new law made life dangerous for runaway black people in the North. They might be found by slavers from the South and returned to the plantations. Returned slaves were beaten harshly to teach them a lesson. Then they were often sold immediately. Their lives, which had been difficult before their journey north, would be much worse from then on.

Not only was the law dangerous to escaped slaves, but whites who helped them were outraged. Now they could be arrested and fined for helping runaway slaves in their own free states!

Since most of the sympathetic white folks who helped runaways did so because they believed they were fighting evil, they felt more anger than fear. They knew that, unlike their black brothers and sisters in Christ, they themselves would never be owned or whipped or sold. They also knew that this

RETURNED SLAVES WERE BEATEN HARSHLY.

new law was immoral and had nothing to do with the laws of God or the love of Christ. So they felt no responsibility to obey it.

Stories began cropping up of whole communities defying the new law and rescuing captured slaves before they could be returned to the South. A few manhunters from the South were no match for a group of angry townspeople. Some slaves were spared in this way and sent on to Canada, where there was no such thing as a Fugitive Slave Law.

It was good to have some white folks on your side, but Harriet knew this law meant more trouble. Now there was no place in America where slaves could escape and live without looking over their shoulders all the time. She'd have to look into what could be done in Canada.

In the meantime, she continued her rescue work. Early in 1851, Harriet returned to her home county in Maryland to escort three slaves, one of them her brother, to Philadelphia. She went back again in the fall to the plantation owned by the

SOME SLAVES WERE SENT ON TO CANADA.

doctor where she had lived. Harriet, dressed in a man's suit and hat, planned to persuade her beloved husband to come away with her.

Of course Harriet had not seen or been in touch with her husband for two years. But she had dreamed of him constantly and truly believed he must miss her as much as she missed him. She was certain John would happily go north with her.

Harriet, who was otherwise so sensible and keenly observant of the world around her, seemed not to be able to see John clearly. Even though he had threatened to betray her—an action that could have cost her her life—Harriet had a forgiving heart. She was still deeply in love with her husband. Time had passed. Surely he would be sorry he had been so stubborn and want to come with her, his own wife.

One night Harriet stood outside the cabin she had shared with John and knocked on the door.

"Someone's knocking, John," a voice said from inside. The voice belonged to someone unmistakably female.

HARRIET KNOCKED ON THE DOOR.

HARRIET TUBMAN

John Tubman opened the door, looking as big and handsome as ever. Harriet stared up at him for a moment, speechless. Then she saw a beautiful young woman standing next to him. Harriet suddenly felt ugly and demeaned.

At first John didn't recognize Harriet in her men's clothes. "Yes?" he said politely. Then he bent down and peered under her hat. "Harriet?" he said in a shocked voice. "Is that you?"

"This is Harriet?" the woman next to him said, disdain in her voice.

John began to laugh. "It sure is. Woman, what you doing dressed like that?" He laughed harder.

Harriet summoned up a smile. "I came back to take you with me, John."

"You what?" John stopped laughing for a moment. "I ain't heard from you in two years. Far as I knew, you were dead. Did you think I was just gonna wait for you?"

"But John—" Harriet began.

John interrupted her.

JOHN BEGAN TO LAUGH.

"You been out of the picture a long time now. You and me are over. I got me a new wife right here, Harriet. We jumped the broom together just last summer. My life is better than ever."

"But John—"

Harriet's protest was drowned out as John erupted into laughter. Then his new wife joined in. Without another word, Mr. and Mrs. John Tubman shut the door, leaving Harriet humiliated and alone in the dark.

Later in the woods, she thought things over. She felt such a wild bunch of emotions—love mixed with hate, sadness mixed with anger, awareness mixed with confusion. John was no longer hers. He had dismissed their marriage vows. He did not love her anymore.

As she mulled that over, Harriet realized that John had shown what he was made of back when she first spoke to him of escape. Clearly he hadn't loved her, even then. Wouldn't a husband want to protect his wife? Why had she thought he'd changed? How

IN THE WOODS, SHE THOUGHT THINGS OVER.

could she have risked her life—her entire mission—
to come to him? He could still be a danger to her.

The worst thought of all for Harriet, though,
was that part of her dream of freedom had included
having John by her side. Now that dream had been
killed by John himself. He could not have told her
more clearly that he had no desire to be part of her
life. He had taken another wife without even trying
to find her.

Harriet cried softly in the woods. Then she
slipped to her knees and prayed. After some time
with the Lord, Harriet's wild emotions subsided to a
dull ache. She knew the emptiness she was feeling
inside would be with her for a long time. But for
now, she had a mission. She was here in territory
she knew. Surely there must be some slaves eager to
escape.

There were. She gathered them that night, and
together they made their way to Philadelphia.

With the effects of the Fugitive Slave Law making themselves seen, and with the death of her

THEY MADE THEIR WAY TO PHILADELPHIA.

dream of married life with John, Harriet threw herself into her mission of freeing her family and anyone else who wanted to escape.

She continued to make trips to the South. She found ways to guide slaves out of Maryland without going with them by drawing maps on their cabins' dirt floors. She had them memorize the stops they would need to take. She only escorted the more difficult or complicated groups.

With this method, Harriet was able to help more slaves escape. Her instructions were so good and her routes so fail-safe, nobody was ever caught. She gained a reputation. People called her Moses. When a throaty voice from someone who could not be seen started singing a soft rendition of "Go Down, Moses" in the quarters, people knew Harriet Tubman was around and willing to help them escape that very night.

Sometimes they heard a strong birdcall and realized that it wasn't the season for such birds to call. Then they knew Moses was around. The next

SHE DREW MAPS ON THEIR CABINS' DIRT FLOORS.

morning, several slaves would be missing.

Harriet had gotten very good at making the journey north. Not only did she know the way and the stations well, she stayed in constant prayer so that her concentration was keen and her inner spirit alert to the suggestions of the Holy Spirit. This was especially important when she was being chased. It was frightening for runaways to hear the sounds of bloodhounds and horses, but Harriet would softly sing, "Wade in the water, wade in the water, children," to get the group into the river where their scent would be lost.

And sometimes she just knew things she should have had no way of knowing. She'd find a way to keep her "passengers" safe.

Once going north, she sensed they were in immediate danger. She put everyone on a south-bound train to throw their pursuers off their trail. After all, who would expect runaway slaves to be heading south? And on a train, no less.

She was creative, too. Wanting to spirit away

IN THE RIVER, THEIR SCENT WOULD BE LOST.

more slaves from her former plantation, she once disguised herself as an old granny slave with a ragged dress and a scarf draped over her head to keep the sun off. She bought several live chickens, which she carried, then she slouched down like a doddering old woman and hobbled down the road in broad daylight.

Of all people, who should ride up the road on his horse but the doctor, her former master! Surely he would see the prominent scar on her face. Quickly, Harriet let go of the chickens so that they squawked and ran and half-flew every which way. Then waddling and bent over like an old woman, she chased after each one. The doctor watched for a while, chuckling as he rode on.

Sometimes the very thing she worried over happened. She would have a seizure and fall into a deep sleep while trying to run slaves out of danger. But during this sleep, she had vivid dreams about what they should do and where they should go when she woke up. Harriet always obeyed these visions, even

HARRIET LET *GO* OF THE CHICKENS.

when they didn't seem to make sense. She believed they came from God.

Usually while on the run, Harriet and her passengers slept by day and traveled by night. But one morning as they were settling down to rest in the forest, one of Harriet's dreams told her they had to keep moving all day. The slavers were on their trail.

She woke everyone up and got them going again. Then she passed out in plain sight in the middle of a road. When she woke up, her passengers were waiting for her out there on that road, the sun shining down on all of them! Harriet was horrified that they could have been seen.

But they hadn't been seen, and Harriet's dream showed her that the bloodhounds were close. She ran everyone back into the woods and zigzagged in every direction until they reached a river. Even though she didn't know this particular river, it had been in her dream. And in the dream, she'd been shown that it had a sandbar on which they could cross.

The others were skeptical, but they had to trust

THE SLAVERS WERE ON THEIR TRAIL.

Harriet. She started across the icy river, all five feet of her. Even though she waded up to her neck, the water never got any deeper. Sure enough, they got to the other side. Eventually they found themselves on an island where Harriet ran them through the woods until they came upon a cabin.

Would the inhabitants be friend or foe? Not to worry. Harriet had seen this in her dream, too. She knocked on the door, and a good Christian family of free blacks answered. There the runaways were able to rest and eat and dry their clothes by the fire.

The next day, they got back to the road by a different route. By noticing trampled grass, cigarette butts, and "Wanted" posters, they realized that the law had tracked them down right to the very spot where Harriet had passed out. The bloodhounds had indeed been on their trail, but the zigzagging had confused them. Then the scent of the runaways had been washed away in the river. The dogs could not find them.

Sometimes a slave was too frightened or too

THE DOGS COULD NOT FIND THEM.

exhausted to go on. But Harriet made that person go on for the sake of everyone else in the group. If even one slave turned back, the law would find ways to make that person talk. The entire Underground Railroad would be jeopardized for both black and white people. Black folks would be sent back to their masters, and white folks would be thrown into prison.

Because of this, Harriet always carried a gun. She prayed she would never have to use it, but when a slave threatened to turn back, she aimed the gun straight at the slave and said with absolute conviction in her voice: "Go free or die." The slave never turned back after that.

And God was merciful. In all her years as a conductor for the Underground Railroad, Harriet never pulled the trigger of her gun.

"GO FREE OR DIE."

THERE WERE ELEVEN IN THE GROUP.

8

As time went on, Harriet knew she needed to take her charges beyond northern states and into Canada. Because of the Fugitive Slave Law and because Philadelphia was so often the stopping place for runaways, that city was no longer safe for escaped slaves.

Her first group of passengers to go to Canada started their journey just as winter hit. This trip took most of December to make, partly because there were eleven in the group. That was more people than Harriet had ever taken north at one time.

Since they were going farther and traveling during winter weather, it took longer than usual. It was not easy to keep such a large group going, fed, rested, and cheered.

For some time the eleven fugitives hid with the great Frederick Douglass in cold and snowy Rochester, New York, near the Canadian border. Douglass was an escaped slave who was both educated and eloquent. He wrote letters and essays and made stirring speeches against slavery, which made him what was called an abolitionist. He and Harriet had tremendous respect for one another's work. He housed her large group for as long as it took to get money and provisions for them to pass safely into Canada.

Though much of the trip was on foot or by boat or wagon, during the last leg of the journey into Canada, the runaways were hidden in the baggage car of a train. Once the train crossed into Canada, the phenomenal Niagara Falls was in sight. And Niagara Falls meant they were in absolutely free territory.

THE FUGITIVES HID WITH FREDERICK DOUGLASS.

Then the fugitives left the baggage car and sat in coach class, watching the mighty roaring waters and softly singing songs of thanks to God.

Harriet's group of eleven people headed toward the town of St. Catherines in Ontario, Canada. Many other ex-slaves lived there, enjoying not only free lives but full lives. They could even vote. Harriet began taking all her groups to St. Catherines, one group every spring, one group every fall.

In 1854, Harriet began having unnerving dreams about three of her brothers back in Maryland. She dreamed they were being sold to the chain gang. She knew what these dreams meant. Her brothers desperately needed to get out of Maryland. She prayed for a way to get a message to them that they must watch for her and come with her on her next journey.

Harriet remembered a free black man back in Maryland named Jacob who could read and write. Jacob knew Harriet's brothers. Jacob's adopted son lived in the North and sent letters to Jacob from time

HARRIET BEGAN HAVING DREAMS ABOUT
THREE OF HER BROTHERS.

to time, so Harriet asked a friend to pen a letter to Jacob under the adopted son's name. She certainly couldn't use her own name, since she was wanted by the law in the South.

But secrecy was necessary for another reason. Local postmasters would open the mail of freed blacks. If there was something considered dangerous or illegal in a letter, Jacob could get in trouble.

The letter was worded carefully so that Jacob would understand that Harriet was coming to get her brothers. It read: "Tell my brothers to be always watching unto prayer, and when the good old ship of Zion comes along, to be ready to step on board." It was signed as if it were from Jacob's adopted son.

The postal authorities gave Jacob the letter and watched him read it. Jacob pretended to read it slowly and with much difficulty, though he'd read it quickly right away. Jacob knew his son had no brothers. There were other clues that told him the letter was not from his son but still intended for Jacob to read. He memorized its words, then told

THE POSTAL AUTHORITIES GAVE JACOB THE LETTER.

the postal authorities that he didn't understand a word of it and handed it back to them.

Jacob had already heard from a reliable source that Harriet's brothers were going to be sold with a lot of other slaves very soon. So he got to the brothers just as fast as he could to tell them that Harriet would be coming for them.

Harriet arrived in December. She got her group together and gathered supplies. Traveling north with her this time would be her brothers Benjamin, William Henry, and John. Also in this group were William Henry's fiancée, Jane Kane, who had dressed in a boy's clothes, and two non-relatives, Peter Jackson and John Chase.

When it was time to leave, Harriet's brother John Ross was not to be found. "I'll leave word how he can find us," Harriet told the others. "We don't wait." She left word with Jacob, then she took her group to the plantation where her parents lived.

They spent Christmas Day hiding in the feed house near her parents' cabin where, blindfolded so

THEY SPENT CHRISTMAS DAY HIDING.

that he could say he never saw his runaway children, Poppa Ross loaded them down with holiday food.

It was at the feed house where John Ross caught up with them, greatly agitated. He hadn't joined them earlier because his wife, Ann, had gone into labor. He wouldn't abandon her, and he ran for the midwife. Their child was born safely. John had left his wife and new baby, both of them crying. He knew that he would have been sold after Christmas anyway and separated from his family. At least this way he could promise his weeping wife that Harriet would come back for her next time.

The band of runaways made it safely north. And Harriet did return to bring back her sister-in-law, the baby, and another child of John and Ann's. When passengers were babies, Harriet would give them a small dose of paregoric, a drug people in the 1800s used as a painkiller. She knew how much to use to keep the baby sleeping but not harm it. Babies never slowed the journey down.

BABIES NEVER SLOWED THE JOURNEY DOWN.

HARRIET TUBMAN

In 1857, Harriet determined that it was time to move her parents north. All her relatives had made it but them. And she'd been having disturbing dreams that those two old folks were about to be sold. In fact, her father was being interrogated almost daily by a plantation owner and the doctor for feeding a runaway. Since Poppa was clever, he was able to say honestly that he hadn't seen the run-away. (It had, after all, been a dark night when he'd fed him, and he had not been able to see him.) And since Poppa had a reputation for honesty, the doctor believed him. But who knew how long the doctor's trust would last?

Harriet's folks were old and arthritic. She knew they could not stand being separated from each other if they were sold. The time had come for action.

Harriet went south, journeyed to the plantation where her parents lived, and waited until dark to approach the cabin. Her parents were thrilled to see her. Poppa was still in trouble, and Momma was wor-ried sick about it. Both of them moved so slowly.

HER PARENTS WERE THRILLED TO SEE HER.

Harriet knew they could not escape on foot.

With her wisdom and daring, Harriet was able to find a horse and wagon. They loaded Momma's feather mattress in it, and off they went, traveling by night, sleeping in the wagon in the woods by day. Once they got out of Maryland and off the wagon, things got easier, and the trip to Canada was uneventful.

But Canadian weather was too extreme for the old folks. They were housebound in the winter and homesick, too. Harriet could see that they would not live long if she didn't provide a different home for them.

In spite of the Fugitive Slave Law and the fact that there was a high reward offered for her capture, Harriet moved her parents into New York. She doubted the bounty hunters would travel that far looking for two elderly slaves who could hardly walk. She bought them a house at 180 South Street in Auburn, New York, while she herself moved back to Canada. The winters in Auburn were rough, too, but

THEY SLEPT IN THE WAGON IN THE WOODS BY DAY.

they were milder than those in St. Catherines. Harriet continued to work to pay the mortgage on her parents' house and to bring more slaves to freedom.

During these years, Harriet began getting to know abolitionists in Boston. She also met John Brown, a compelling but disturbed white abolitionist who would later murder his way across the country in an attempt to free slaves. Harriet appreciated John Brown's insistence that slaves must be freed immediately, but she never agreed with using violence. So Harriet Tubman and John Brown never worked together.

But Harriet did, at the encouragement of other northern abolitionists, begin speaking to groups about slavery. She told of the great risks slaves would take simply to be free, how they traveled under cover of darkness on foot with only the North Star to guide them. She spoke of her mission from the Lord. She relayed true stories of the Underground Railroad and was a compelling speaker with her deep and husky voice.

SHE MET JOHN BROWN.

HARRIET TUBMAN

The fact that she sometimes lay right down and fell into deep sleep in the middle of a speech did not keep crowds from coming to hear her speak. When she'd wake up, she'd simply begin speaking from where she'd left off. Harriet became a popular speaker.

One day she had a horrible intuition that something was wrong with John Brown. She could not shake the evil feeling. Later she learned that John Brown and his gang had seized a government arsenal at Harper's Ferry to help free slaves. In the standoff that ensued, many people were killed. John Brown survived, was put on trial, sentenced to death, and executed. Harriet wished violence had not been a part of John Brown's misguided plans for liberty.

The incident at Harper's Ferry was one of many that divided the opinions of the North and the South on the subject of slavery. Many in the North saw John Brown as a martyr. Many in the South felt even more threatened by their own slaves. Something tragic was bound to happen.

JOHN BROWN AND HIS GANG
SEIZED A GOVERNMENT ARSENAL.

IN 1861, THE CIVIL WAR BEGAN.

9

In 1861, the Civil War began, a bloody struggle between the northern and southern states of America. Much of what started this war was about the institution of slavery. The South needed slaves to continue its way of life. The North wanted the South to rid itself of slavery. Which side would win?

During the war, Harriet Tubman shifted her efforts. She worked with the Union Army in a fort under Union control in South Carolina. There she nursed sick, starving, and wounded slaves back to health. She searched the area for healing herbs and roots and brewed herbal medicines for them. She saved many lives in her role as nurse, and once again her charges called her Moses.

During this time, Harriet saw her first regiment of all black soldiers marching for the Union. It was a stunning sight. Black folks wept openly as the proud regiment marched by. Harriet quietly praised God that such a day had come, even if it was in a war.

Harriet also worked with the Union Army as a scout and a spy. Having brought slaves out of the South unseen all those years, she was perfectly prepared for such secretive work.

In 1863, she helped an army regiment of former slaves raid a Confederate camp and rescue about eight hundred slaves. They picked the slaves up in small boats and rowed them to huge gunboats, and Harriet sang the old songs to keep the slaves calm. This raid and Harriet's participation in it made front-page news in Boston. The Bostonians loved this courageous woman!

Harriet continued her hospital work for the

HARRIET SAW HER FIRST REGIMENT OF ALL BLACK SOLDIERS.

army throughout the war. After the North claimed victory, the ratification of the Thirteenth Amendment brought an end to the painful era of slavery in the United States.

THE THIRTEENTH AMENDMENT BROUGHT
AN END TO THE ERA OF SLAVERY.

SHE WAS RESPONSIBLE FOR BRINGING
THREE HUNDRED SLAVES TO FREEDOM.

Epilogue

After Harriet Tubman escaped from slavery, she made nineteen more trips into the highly dangerous South. She was responsible for bringing three hundred slaves to freedom. Some were escorted by her. She gave others clear directions. But all of these slaves came face-to-face with the powerful and brave woman they called Moses who led man, woman, and child out of bondage with her throaty songs. As a conductor for the Underground Railroad, she never lost a passenger. They all arrived safely in the North.

HARRIET TUBMAN

During the Civil War raid, Harriet was responsible for rescuing about eight hundred more slaves. Nobody knows how many ex-slaves she saved by nursing them back to health in the camps through the war years.

In total, Harriet Tubman brought well over a thousand slaves to liberty. A true American, Harriet was chosen by God to lead her people to freedom. Not only did she perform these tasks at great personal risk, but she also gave up pleasures, comfort, and security in order to fulfill her mission. For many years, all her money and time were devoted to bringing slaves to freedom.

After the war, Harriet returned to her parents' house in Auburn, New York. There she worked to support her parents, and she continued her speaking engagements. She also spoke in favor of the rights of women, who at that time could not vote or own property.

In 1867, Harriet learned that John Tubman had been murdered in Maryland. Harriet never married

SHE CONTINUED HER SPEAKING ENGAGEMENTS.

again, and she never had children, a rarity among women of the nineteenth century. She never made much money, and what she had, she gave to those in need as Christ tells all Christians to do.

Harriet believed that when we open our homes to the poor, we entertain Christ Himself. So in her later years she fed and housed poor black people in her home. Her house in Auburn, New York, was always open to the needy. She continued to raise money to help others.

In March 1913, Harriet Tubman died in Auburn and was buried in Fort Hill Cemetery. She is believed to have lived ninety-three years, but no one knows for sure when she was born.

In 1978, a postage stamp with her picture was released by the United States Post Office. The citizens of Auburn built Freedom Park, a tribute to Harriet's work in the cause of freedom.

Today Harriet Tubman's house in Auburn is a museum about the Underground Railroad and Harriet Tubman. The house is owned and operated

TODAY HARRIET TUBMAN'S HOUSE IN AUBURN IS A MUSEUM.

by the African Methodist Episcopal Zion Church. Tours are available.

Harriet Tubman is with the Lord now. But while she walked this earth, she devoted her life to what she felt the Lord would have her do.

HARRIET TUBMAN DEVOTED HER LIFE
TO WHAT SHE FELT THE LORD WOULD HAVE HER DO.

AWESOME BOOKS FOR KIDS!

The Young Reader's Christian Library
Action, Adventure, and Fun Reading!

This series for young readers ages 8 to 12 is action-packed, fast-paced, and Christ-centered! With exciting illustrations on every other page following the text, kids won't be able to put these books down! Over 100 illustrations per book. All books are paperbound. The unique size (4 ⅛" x 5 ⅜") makes these books easy to take anywhere!

A Great Selection to Satisfy All Kids!

Abraham Lincoln	Elijah	Miriam
Billy Graham	Esther	Moses
Billy Sunday	Florence Nightingale	Paul
Christopher Columbus	Hudson Taylor	Peter
Clara Barton	In His Steps	The Pilgrim's Progress
Corrie ten Boom	Jesus	Roger Williams
Daniel	Jim Elliot	Ruth
David	Joseph	Samuel
David Brainerd	Little Women	Samuel Morris
David Livingstone	Luis Palau	Sojourner Truth
Deborah	Lydia	
